To Persevere Nonetheless

To Persevere Nonetheless

---⭒---

Letters of Spiritual Direction

By

Fr. Piotr Rostworowski

Translated by Justyna Krukowska

THE CENACLE PRESS
AT SILVERSTREAM PRIORY

Originally published as *Wytrwać wbrew wszystkiemu*
by Klasztor Benedyktynek Sakramentek (Warszawa)
Benedyktynki-Sakramentki, 2022

Copyright © 2023 Silverstream Priory

All rights reserved:
No part of this book may be reproduced or transmitted,
in any form or by any means, without permission.

The Cenacle Press at Silverstream Priory
Silverstream Priory
Stamullen, County Meath, K32 T189, Ireland
www.cenaclepress.com

ppr 978-1-915544-61-2

Book design
by Silverstream Priory
Cover art: Dieric Bouts, *Prophet Elijah in the Desert* (1465)

Introduction

"Spiritual direction is collaboration with the living God in the fulfillment of His designs in people." These words of Father Piotr best describe his philosophy of the ministry he exercised among the many people seeking to advance their spiritual lives. According to his diaries where he recorded all the letters, he wrote a total of 29,702 letters throughout his life. Father Piotr clearly had a gift for writing, although he conceded that writing was "very hard work" for him.

According to Fr. Piotr Rostworowski, "the point of life is to wander into the unknown, through the desert wilderness, where the only chance of reaching your destination without straying into the desert sands is to be completely pliant towards the invisible Wisdom, which leads you by paths known only to her."

Although the letters included in this booklet are short, they have depth, and undoubtedly the soul to whom they were addressed was in need of such concrete and firm guidance. As a result, they can become a comprehensive message for anyone experiencing spiritual warfare and wishing to cultivate and maintain a living relationship with God.

Bielany, May 18, 1968

Dear Sister,

I found your letter upon my return from the Shrine of Our Lady of Częstochowa. I read it carefully and it actually made me happy. I see that despite this whole crisis, God is keeping you firmly by His side and not letting go.

You belong to Him, and this horrible battle you are experiencing is the consequence of that. It is a battle between His grace and the pride that you have not yet vanquished in yourself.

I understand you feel great difficulty and resistance whenever you contemplate forcing yourself to apologize to Mother. No wonder, because a great victory is usually very hard; very hard, but also very valuable. However, I can't plead with you and beg you hard enough not to retreat from this difficult act of humility and fortitude, but to make this sacrifice of love to the Lord Jesus and to open more room for Him in your clenched soul. Indeed, my child, this is a crucial task that you can accomplish right now.

I very much count on you and on the great good that is within you despite all the hardness of your character. I request the assistance of your prayers and your sacrifice, and I bless you with all my heart.

Yours in the Lord,

Father

February 5, 1972

Dear Sister,

Your letter pleased me all the same. This painful state in which you are finding yourself, and from which you are unsuccessfully attempting to flee, does not imply a regression at all, but on the contrary, it signifies progress, even though everything within you is proclaiming the opposite.

However, you would not possess such a knowledge or perception of your own wretchedness, nor such a loathing for your conduct, nor such a desire for God and holiness, had He not worked in you and illuminated your darkness with His invisible light.

On the contrary, you would perhaps have a predilection for yourself, and your desires would be directed towards the things of this world.

Do not flee but rather remain quietly in your monastery. Nor should you run away from this inner pain, or defend yourself against the light that accuses you, but accept this just accusation, humble yourself inwardly and beg for mercy, for the grace to do His will eternally, and for the gift of His Spirit.

As the warm blood pushes its way to the body's frozen members, it is accompanied by a sharp pain, but this pain is better than the loss of feeling that precedes it, because means that life is returning.

So it is with your soul. The One to whom you were unfaithful has not stopped loving you. He is unfailingly faithful, and He took seriously the sacrifice of your vows, in which He Himself was personally involved. Now he is undertaking the task of healing you, despite everything. You are on His operating table and the surgery has already begun. You have to surrender all the way to the end.

May Christ bless you!

Yours in Him,

Father

Bielany, December 31, 1973

Dear Sister,

Your prayer is not without merit at all, but you must persevere. It is so dry that you can't feel it at all, and instead you feel that something is being ripped apart and that you are being unfaithful to someone when you cut your prayer short and walk away.

And yet your vocation is the vocation to prayer, to adoration and to that difficult but real contact with God, in whom alone lies that simple, yet difficult, solution to the problem of your soul. This is what you must fight for until the end, because this is truly your calling, outside of which you will find no meaning and will crumble. The Lord is calling you to this encounter with Him, wherein lie your salvation and your transformation.

Do not therefore complicate your problem unnecessarily, but with all your might be faithful to this encounter and do not flee the site of this encounter, but instead persevere. He will not leave you like this without any help, and you already have the grace of true prayer, despite these difficulties and doubts.

When it comes to spiritual direction, stay simple and pay no heed to how they are treating you. That has nothing to do with it. If we seek the truth, it matters not in what packaging it comes. To think otherwise is to succumb to the sulking of pride, which can rob us of great goods. I entrust you to God's care in this New Year.

Your loving Father

Bieniszew, July 12, 1974

Dear Sister,

I received your letter, enclosed here, shortly before my trip abroad. I have now returned and I am sending the letter back to you so that you can re-read it to yourself, as I think you have already dealt with the difficulties mentioned in it, which are quite normal in a person's life.

We must think more about what we should do to extend kindness to the Sisters than about what unpleasant things we suffer from the Sisters or Superiors. Such thinking is futile and brings the soul no benefit, just harm.

You need some fortitude and patience. This virtue is especially necessary for us on this earth, as without it we will not get very far.

My blessings as you practice this virtue.

May the peace of God be with you!

Father

Bielany, December 30, 1974

Dear Sister,

Having known your soul for a very long time, I can say that you are on the right path. It is a difficult path, because you have a difficult and impetuous disposition, and thus a character that is difficult to groom. However, you have already come to know yourself and are able to look soberly and critically at the stirrings of rebellion to which you used to succumb indiscriminately.

Keep working, praying, and trusting, because your collaboration with grace is not and will not be in vain.

Silence is good for you, but I don't think that such a complete separation from all spiritual guidance and all supervision is salutary for you. I think you should have a priest to whom you could reveal your soul. Then other confidences would no longer be necessary. With your personality, however, you can't shut yourself off, that wouldn't be good.

Pray that God will send you such help. I am counting on your prayer support.

Yours in the Lord,

Father

Bieniszew, May 25, 1975

ear Sister,

I think you should not switch your confessor, but continue to go to Father N. Sisters should not get involved in these matters. The reasons you mention are not serious enough to justify such a change.

Thank you for the prayer support.

In Christo,

Father

Bielany, August 4, 1975

Dear Sister,

Forgive me for only responding to your letter today. I was awfully swamped with work for the whole of July. I was very happy to hear your news. May God give you the grace to persevere in your excellent retreat resolutions. It was He who gave you the light to see the road you should take to Him.

I wish you this faithful, quiet collaboration with His grace that brings victory.

Yours in the Lord,

Father

BIELANY, JUNE 14, 1976

Dear Sister,

So many different letters and various affairs are awaiting my response that I still have not replied to your letter, although I took it with me to Bieniszew.

Let me start with a less important matter: I think that if the congregation has adopted cross necklaces and the vast majority of Sisters wear them, there is no rationale for continuing with the monstrance necklaces. Adopting the new necklace is more conducive to unity and peace in the religious family. Besides, a cross makes more sense than a monstrance, which does not symbolize Eucharistic adoration, but merely represents the ecclesiastical vessel used to expose the Blessed Sacrament.

Regarding your inner life, it seems to me that in the absence of any consolation there some divine action is cleansing your soul, which must be endured with humility and patience, and any quest for recompense in some inferior gratifications must be avoided. You must remain in this "vacuum" as long as God wills it. Such an attitude will not tarnish God's action by introducing our own. God knows what He is doing. He is good and He will not let you perish.

The soul may easily sink into terror in this state,

believing that it is becoming indifferent to everything, that it is losing its spirituality, and sinking further and further into darkness and nothingness.

You must not be afraid, you simply have to trust and persevere. I think there is nothing wiser that you can do, and the Lord will do His part.

I entrust myself to your kind prayers.

Yours in Lord Jesus,

Father

Bielany, December 30, 1976

Dear Sister,

If God permits, I will be in Warsaw on the 18th of January. I would like to come and visit the Sisters around 3 pm.

In Christo,

Father

Bielany, Easter of 1977

ear Sister,

The Lord Jesus will come in the glory of the Resurrection and will tell us: "Peace be unto you!" If you open your soul, this ineffable peace will flow into its depths as well. You will then understand the triviality of many things.

Superiors also have the right to be wrong, they have the right to make mistakes, because they are human just like we are.

Our deep and forgiving kindness towards them will solve many difficulties and allow us to live in peace.

Yours in the love of God,

Father

Bielany, February 5, 1978

Dear Sister,

My heartfelt congratulations on your anniversary. These 25 years that you have spent in the monastery are God's immense grace. I say grace, because it was given to me to know and follow its work in your rather recalcitrant soul. We should give thanks to God that He has not let you out of His hand!

I am also thankful for you and for your perseverance despite everything, cooperating with God through so many challenging moments. There are times in our lives when we can think of nothing wiser than to persevere nonetheless.

I understand your resistance to the different changes introduced into monastic life in recent times. Indeed, a lot of naturalism has entered it, and a lot of monastic politics. Something of our former austere simplicity has been lost.

Weekly confession is nowadays suppressed as an obligation, but not as an option, and there would be no harm in it if the confessors, who come every other week, did not all come on the same day. You can also go to confession with another priest who comes to visit, or with a chaplain.

May the peace of the Lord be with you always! I cordially bless you in God's Name.

Yours in Lord Jesus,

Father

BIELANY, EASTER OF 1978

Dear Sister,

Thanks for your letter. We must thank God, who knows how to subdue the wayward and defiant souls with His love!

I saw from the beginning that you have God's calling, but that the battle would be tough!

Sometimes a big pike will swallow the bait, but the fisherman will have to work hard before he can subdue it and get it out of the water, because it's a tough catch.

I have been witnessing this marvelous goodness and patience of God towards your soul. Therefore, today I am rejoicing with you.

Yours in Lord Jesus,

Father

Bieniszew, July 18, 1978

I have no knowledge of what feelings your Mother Superior harbors towards Mother N., but her unwillingness to let either of you go to X. is perfectly understandable, because the kind of life they are living in X. is not suitable for you and is not compatible with your vocation.

As for this inner emptiness and resentment that you are experiencing, always remember that the ordinary way of spiritual life was revealed to us by God in the Book of Exodus, in the journey of the Israelites through the desert to the promised land.

Springs of living water were very scarce there, instead it was just sand all around. At times they also felt like going back to Egypt, but some of them put their trust in the Lord, "No man putting his hand to the plough, and looking back, is fit for the kingdom of God… but he that shall persevere unto the end, he shall be saved." Thanks for your greetings!

Peace to you,

Father

BIENISZEW, JANUARY 10, 1979

Dear Sister,

Your lot seems to be that of suffering numerous temptations. You will prevail over them as you proceed with simplicity, following the Rule. The devil is terribly afraid of this simplicity, because it makes him lose his foothold.

Your doubts regarding both the desire to leave and the monstrance pendant are addressed by Saint Benedict in his eighth step of humility. If you are earnestly seeking the answer, you will find it there.

There is no other way for you but to persevere in the monastery until the end, which will not be long now.

The Israelites' march through the desert is the revealed model for our lives. Oases and springs of living water were scarce there. The Israelites were mostly surrounded by bare rocks and sands all around.

And yet, the only wisdom they had was to keep marching...

Blessings,

Father

Bieniszew, December 12, 1979

Dear Sister,

I think you are taking a very good path, but the Lord must discipline such a hard-headed soul.

This is the way the Scriptures show us in Exodus and Numbers, which are the typological teachings modeling Christian life to us. It is a march through the wilderness, where springs are scarce and the daily experience is just sand, sand and even more sand.

But this path is a sure one. I don't see any reason why you should change your confessor. I believe it is a temptation.

I send you my blessings and entrust you to Our Lady.

Please assist me with your prayers,

Father

BIENISZEW, DECEMBER 23, 1980

Dear Sister,

We are guided by faith, and by the power of faith we can conquer all things and "extinguish all the fiery darts of the most wicked one", if we only ask.

We are not guided by feelings. Obviously, every community has its strong and weak points. But we have come to love this community and through it we are growing into the Church and into Christ. This is enough for us, if we believe. We don't need to focus either on our feelings, or on how the Sisters are treating us, but instead we should focus on doing a little more good in this world, showing a little more kindness to the Sisters, spreading a little more of God's love in this world, maybe suffering a little more and then – we should get on our way. Remember, your time is short! It doesn't matter what you are feeling or what you are experiencing, but it matters what you have left to do and what good you still can do. Think about it.

The cloister is not a goal, but rather an important commitment and part of our witness to the Church and to the world as a sign of the Lord's exclusive love. Therefore, in order to ask for a dispensation from the cloister, there must be a really important reason. If mom were to absolutely need your help, that would be a pretty compelling reason, but if there is no such necessity, then the commitment to the cloister should be maintained.

Blessings,

Father

Bieniszew, December 27, 1981

Dear Sister,

I am very glad that God is clearly drawing you to Himself, because it is definitely He. Strive to be meekly submissive to His grace and use your retreat to that end.

Do not let external things provoke you to intervene. These are temptations meant to distract you from your work in order to scatter the great good that is born of God's love.

Thank you for your prayers. I am almost fine now, but I am still on a liquid-only diet because of the jaws healing.

May the peace of God be with you!

Blessings,

Father

About The Cenacle Press
at Silverstream Priory

An apostolate of the Benedictine monastery of Silverstream Priory in Ireland, the mission of The Cenacle Press can be summed up in four words: Quis ostendit nobis bona—who will show us good things (Psalm 4:6)? In an age of confusion, ugliness, and sin, our aim is to show something of the Highest Good to every reader who picks up our books. More specifically, we believe that the treasury of the centuries-old Benedictine tradition and the beauty of holiness which has characterized so many of its followers through the ages has something beneficial, worthwhile, and encouraging in it for every believer.

cenaclepress.com

Also available from The Cenacle Press
at Silverstream Priory

Robert Hugh Benson

The King's Achievement
By What Authority
The Friendship of Christ
Papers of a Pariah
Christ in the Church

Bl Columba Marmion

Christ the Ideal of the Monk
Christ in His Mysteries
Words of Life On the Margin of the Missal

Dom Pius De Hemptinne

A Benedictine Soul: Biography, Letters, and Spiritual Writings of Dom Pius De Hemptinne

Dom Hubert Van Zeller

Letters to A Soul
Approach to Penance
Approach to Monastcisim
Sanctity in Other Words
The Yoke of Divine Love

Dom Eugene Vandeur

Hail Mary

Father Ryan T Sliwa

New Nazareth's In Us

Monks of Silverstream Priory

Dawn Tears, Spring Light, Rood Peace: Poems

cenaclepress.com

www.ingramcontent.com/pod-product-compliance
Lightning Source LLC
Chambersburg PA
CBHW030046100526
44590CB00011B/346